# THE NAME MUSEUM

Winner of the De Novo Poetry Prize

Copyright © 2014 Nick McRae

All rights reserved

Printed in the United States of America

First Edition

No part of this book may be reproduced or used in any form or by any means without written permission from the publisher.

ISBN: 978-193-619617-3
LCCN: 2013958053

C&R Press
812 Westwood Ave. Suite D
Chattanooga TN 37405
www.crpress.org


Cover Art: Debora Greger
Book Design: John Estes

# The Name Museum

## Nick McRae

# CONTENTS

The Name Museum     5

I.

Psalm 137     9
Thanatophobia on Shinbone Valley Road     10
For the Robinson Brothers
    of Chattooga County, Georgia, Now Deceased     12
Mountain Redemption     13
Genesis     15
Joseph Van Gilreath (1924–1991)     16
Killing A Rattler     17
Gutting the Farmhouse Upon Grandfather's Death
    from Alzheimer's     18
Beheaded Carcass of a Deer     19
Cozy Manor Personal Care Home,
    LaFayette, Georgia     20
Drawl     21
Apple     22
Persimmon     23
Deacons Meeting     24
Take, Eat     25

II.

Jaroslav Seifert Praying     29
Martin, Slovakia     30
Moravia     31
Prayer     32
Foreigners     33
Introduction to Czech Studies     41
Not Recognizing the Stone Is a Lion     43
Benediction for Slovakia     44

III.
| | |
|---|---|
| Isaiah | 49 |
| Forgiveness | 50 |
| Pessimist's Guide to Miracles | 51 |
| St. Nicholas of Lycia, Defender of Orthodoxy, Wonderworker | 52 |
| Czar Nicholas the Bloody | 53 |
| Nicolas of Antioch, the Proselyte | 54 |
| Nicholas Copernicus | 55 |
| The Last Sheep in Uz | 56 |
| Something Else | 57 |
| Of Solomon | 58 |
| Samson in Love | 59 |
| An Email from God Concerning the Recent Plague of Locusts | 60 |
| The Apocalypse Blahs | 62 |
| Orpheus in Huntsville, Alabama | 64 |
| Seminarian at the Preachers' Convention | 65 |

Notes
Acknowledgments

*For Chad Davidson & Andrew Hudgins*

*For he seeth that wise men die, likewise the fool and the brutish person perish, and leave their wealth to others.*

*Their inward thought is, that their houses shall continue for ever, and their dwelling places to all generations; they call their lands after their own names.*

*Nevertheless man being in honour abideth not: he is like the beasts that perish.*

—Psalm 49:10–12

# THE NAME MUSEUM

Mine was just inside the foyer, between the ficus
in its Greco-Roman plasticware and the rack
of local brochures, one promising the best pad thai
in town, and I knew that it was.
We were members, both of us, and so we headed
straight through the velvet ropes, past the ticket vendor
dozing in his glass box, to the vaulted chamber
of Charles, the plaster and gold foil
flaking now with age. I wanted to tear through the place,
down the halls centuries long, but you held me by the wrist,
gestured like a docent toward each name as we passed.
Catherine: Queen of England, film star, the saint
whose reliquaried head we saw boxed in Siena,
your grandmother. David: Psalmist, Scottish philosopher,
Michelangelo's passion, the man you once made love to
on the shore of Lake Superior in early autumn,
bathed in headlights and dark flannel.
Tristan: no one is really called Tristan.
Yours had a room of its own—small, tasteful
in that Continental sort of way, all soft lines and pastels.
You had always thought it would be bigger,
would house a string quartet to play your name
like a fugue, like a wedding song.

I.

# PSALM 137

*for my grandfathers*

Where now are the old men of my childhood
    who laughed, swore, jawed plugs of tobacco
    and spat the red-brown swill into the dust
     while their wives lined pews and threw their bodies
    on the altar, wailing, *I will cling to the old rugged cross*
    *and exchange it someday for a crown*?
Where are the men who pressed through briars
    and barbed wire, scoured close-grown pine woods
    for winter calves, heaved the bleating beasts
    onto their shoulders and trudged through frost
    as hot piss trickled down their backs?
Where are the young men who, elbow deep in grease,
    leaned, blackened, into the shells of Internationals,
    knuckles bloodied, and tooled the cast-iron
    carcasses to life?
Where are the boys who strung up two-point bucks
    by kerosene light, sliced the creatures throat to groin,
    and flushed out the steaming viscera?
Where are the children who squatted by creeks
    in dark pine thickets, hovered over the waters,
    dragged their fingers through loose silt,
    feeling for the delicate forms of crawdads and tadpoles—
    who tore through briars with wild abandon
    and sprang forth bleeding, laughing, swatting mosquitoes
    from their necks and picking burrs from their hair—
    who, bodies light and scrubbed red, dozed through hymns
    and sermons on thick-aired church days and woke
    to the sobs of old women while the organ droned?
Where, O Lord, is the home I only almost had—
    mythic, bloody as a psalm in the mouths
    of old and dying men who will take it
    with them wholly when they go?

# THANATOPHOBIA ON SHINBONE VALLEY ROAD

Dearest fawn,
              half-crushed
on the pavement, forgive me.

Having found you already
dying, panting, feebly hoofing the asphalt,
unable to crawl away
from your back end—

limp, twisted, varnishing
itself in black-red,
hide gashed and mottled, light
fur thickly matted—

what my father once called mercy
I can't set my hand to,

can't raise the barrel,
send you leadenly into
the after, where nothing awaits us.

Life has been hard. It will yet be worse.
For this, I am sorry.

Yesterday, my father brought me
two halves of a rattlesnake—

one gripped by the rattler, the other
the head.
The pieces swayed in the wind.

*This is what happens*, he said,
and said nothing else.

This is what happens, fawn.
Nothing else.
I don't want to believe that.

The weather is nice today, and it will be
a long time before I die.

## FOR THE ROBINSON BROTHERS OF CHATTOOGA COUNTY, GEORGIA, NOW DECEASED

Old women called the two's affliction *meanness*—
a word they usually saved for naughty children—
for these were Robinsons, not normal folk,
and couldn't help themselves.
                                  In Center Post,
in Harrisburg, and far away as Gore
or Welcome Hill, god-fearing gossips clucked
and spun the brothers' mischief into tales:
one brother'd gone out whoring on a Sunday
while the other, drunk on cheap corn liquor,
fired his twelve-gauge at the Piggly Wiggly's
porcine marquee and, laughing, made the sheriff
chase him around the block until he spewed.

No one knew the brothers' Christian names
or which pine-dotted holler they called home.
Folks didn't know the older brother wept
when, on the radio, a preacher read
the Psalms, or that he played the fiddle deep
into the nights he once drank his way through—
and no one knew the younger brother'd lost
his wife to shine and almost ate his gun
a time or two.
                    But folks had seen their work,
the fly-swarmed carcasses of deer they'd poached—
the heads severed, meat unharvested,
hides marked with a shaky, knife-scrawled *R*.

# MOUNTAIN REDEMPTION

When Ottis Wilkins lost his arm,
he burned his tiny sawmill down
then sold his long-dead in-laws' farm
and moved his family into town.
He opened up a barber shop
and hired his sons to sweep and mop
the place each day and brew coffee
for the men who came to see
the one-armed barber. Inch by inch,
the fresh-barbed rose up from the seat
like sinners from the mourners' bench.

Petunia Eckert's heart was broken
down and blown out like a tire.
The skinny girl she loved had taken
all Petunia's pluck and fire
and moved to Blue Ridge. Petie took
to church and, Sundays, wailed and shook
and made the preacher smile. That summer
Pete got work as a part-time plumber.
In basements she would flail her wrench
and watch rats, terror-maddened, clamber
like sinners to the mourners' bench.

Old Jackie Raburn didn't hold
with killing. Even the mice and snakes
that shimmied nightly over the cold
stones of Jackie's floors caught breaks
no other man would care to give them.
He had a shotgun, though, one trimmed
with etched brass plates. Some days he'd haul
the thing outside and discharge all
his shells at the ground and blast a trench
in it, then wait for silence to fall
like sinners to the mourners' bench.

Whenever Sheriff Biggers drank,
and that was often, he revved his Chevy's
engine up, sped past the bank
and dingy Main Street shops with a heavy
foot and siren wailing just
to see the townsfolk gawk as the rust-
and dirt-stained cruiser barreled by.
Once, he had to shoot a guy
to death. He watched the man's jaw clench,
his dead eyes lifted to the sky
like sinners' from the mourners' bench.

Preacher Greene, a handsome man,
a widower of just a year,
made all the married women fan
themselves and smile from ear to ear
when he preached of David's lustful pride
or the spear that pierced the Savior's side.
At home, the phone set off the hook,
he'd open to his favorite book—
Song of Songs—then feel the pinch
of chaste Paul's thorn as his fingers shook
like sinners on the mourners' bench.

And mountain people—hard as limestone,
rich as black silt, deep as clay—
dreamed each night of valley towns
where valley cornstalks stood up tall
like sinners from the mourners' bench.

# GENESIS

It may have been a whim on which the world—
the universe—was spoken into matter.
Then we happened and made ourselves the master
of it all—the beautiful and gnarled
collection: root and flesh, baleen and feather.
And it may have been an accident that cast
us all from Paradise into the grassed
and dying fields to hunger, kill, and weather.

But separate as we were—the rise and fall
of towers and tribes, our languages confused,
the rocks we lay our heads on lashed to spears—
we found a covenant in the green sea's swell,
the cypress with its windy voice, a bruised
body entwined with ours, our numbered years.

# JOSEPH VAN GILREATH (1924–1991)

*Having a live coal in his hand, ... he laid it upon my mouth,
and said, Lo, ... thine iniquity is taken away.* —Isaiah 6:6-7

Back from the war, he married
a church girl. Together, they worked
his father's farm until the farm

wouldn't pay, then both took jobs
in the carpet mills that sprang up
like pokeweed across the Georgia foothills.

She called him a tall drink of water.
Long and lithe, he towered over everyone,
though all in those parts came

from the same Scotch-Irish stock—
all Gilreaths, Hoods, McRaes, Littlejohns—
all stooped and copper-haired.

Once he doused a cigarette
on his wife's tongue as, eyes closed,
she stuck it out at him. Weeks later,

the razor hook of his carpet knife slipped
from its work and sank into his eyeball.
He called it his just deserts.

For years, when he fell asleep in his chair,
his glass eye open and glistening as he snored,
he scared the life out of his grandkids.

Like Christ, he was always watching.
On a hot Tuesday, while his old International
idled beneath him, his heart seized.

They found him in the fresh-plowed dirt,
his good eye staring at the sun,
the glass one half-buried in the earth.

# KILLING A RATTLER

At first, the double-barreled shotgun blast,
and then the dull, wet thump and metal clank
the snake made as he dropped it chunk by chunk
into a pail. With eyes clamped shut, I'd missed

the kill. I felt a rough hand clasp my wrist
as his tobacco wafted close: *Boy, think
before you walk out here alone.* The stink
of blood and gunshot ripened as he passed

the pail beneath my face. I'd heard of snakes
the size of a man's leg, been taught to steer
away from brush and dark thickets. I squealed

as Grandpa palmed my forearm like an axe.
He thrust my hand into the cooling mire
of meat and scales then held me as I bawled.

# GUTTING THE FARMHOUSE UPON GRANDFATHER'S DEATH FROM ALZHEIMER'S

My heart leapt when I thought
    of all I could destroy.

I tore the cherry banisters
    from the foyer's broad staircase

and piled the splintered dowels by the door.
    Dad ripped piping from beneath the sink.

The hollow copper rasped and clanged
    as he dropped each length of pipe at his feet.

He raised an axe, cleaved
    each cabinet door from its hinges,

and hurled the ruined wood through
    the window frame he'd emptied with a sledge.

I swung my old claw hammer
    and pierced the drywall.

Jaw clenched, I hammered
    until my arms were rubber,

then followed the floor's vibrations to the pantry
    to watch Dad hoist his sledge and laugh,

smashing the shelves to splinters,
    his eyes full of sweat and rapture.

# BEHEADED CARCASS OF A DEER

We cannot know its pilfered head
with velveteen antlers. And yet its hide
is still imbued with heat from inside
like a living thing, though now it's hours dead.

Otherwise the steam would not still rise
from the neck's stump; the blood pool wouldn't grow
in a widening ring like a red-black halo
on the leaves before my and my father's eyes.

Otherwise our nostrils wouldn't flare
with hate so fresh and mournful, as the deer's
must have flared when the poacher's shot rang out;

when the bullet split the morning air;
when from the woods the deer's death caught our ears.
We drag it homeward: silent, sick, devout.

# COZY MANOR PERSONAL CARE HOME, LAFAYETTE, GEORGIA

The room's too hot and reeks of piss and puke
and lemon bleach. Paw Paw's flannel robe's
stained gold with weak iced tea, his cuff's hem frayed,
picked ragged by his untrimmed fingernails.

The nurse tells Dad he wet the bed again,
says he shakes and hollers in the night
and half the time they have to strap him down.
She says he'll barely touch his collard greens,

his buttermilk and cornbread, honey-softened
saltine crackers—but that he's doing fine.
Every time we leave, Dad doesn't talk
for hours, just grips the steering wheel and stares,

and when he speaks he begs me for his life.
*Don't do that to me, son. Don't never do it.*

# DRAWL

I.

Sweet sorghum on a lover's tongue
Fresh briar marks on her thighs
Black beetles cased in cedar sap
      with new-hatched dragonflies

II.

A knife wound stanched with masking tape
A bin of cottonseed
One boy's fist on another's jaw
Bone shards in chicken feed

III.

What thoroughness    What cleanliness
An altar glazed with wax
Deer trails through the dark pine woods
Abandoned railroad tracks

IV.

On crumpled onionskin the words
      of Christ like sunburn scars
Liquor drawn from sweet corn mash
The black between the stars

# APPLE

A man finds an apple in an empty field,
no tree for miles, only fescue, ankle-high,
yellowed with sun and drought. He holds
the green fruit to his face, smells its tart musk,
feels on his lips the skin's fine grit,
the heat of evenings trapped in its meat.
He thinks of the quince trees he dreamed
under as a boy, stacking the pale fruit,
bulbous, splotched, hard as river rock,
into fragrant pyramids he could topple
with a finger, how he spent whole summers
calculating their paths as they spilled
like seed across the patchy ryegrass.
He remembers the first tooth he lost to one,
a quince, when he first tried for a bite,
remembers the small tearing sound,
the acid taste of blood and fruit, the shock
and then the cool relief as his gasp drew
wind across the wound. But there are no
children in the field, and this sun is nothing
good to dream under, so the man decides
to go on his way. At first he places the apple
like an egg back on its bed of grass,
but then he sees the peel's faint freckles,
the stunning blackness of the shadow it casts
on the turf. He squats before the apple,
lays hands on its warm weight, head bowed,
imagines the bite he would take, feels it sour
in his cheeks. Handful after handful,
he tears the spiny grass from its roots,
parts the soil's black jaws. He rolls the fruit
into the wrist-deep maw, presses sod
down over it, lies upon it bodily, his ear
to the ground, strains to hear it growing,
to hear the deep shade that will bloom
any moment, any moment, surely it will.

# PERSIMMON

As a boy, I built a trap for deer
from rusted tin and bailing twine
and rigged it up between the farm's
last two persimmon trees.
I'd seen the deer Dad strung up in the barn,
strips of hide and organs
strewn among the straw.
When morning came,
the shard of ruined tin hung lifeless
from its net of twine—
the trap untripped.
I laughed and breathed
and hacked the knotted cord
to pieces with my pocketknife,
then made a bed of leaves
and ate my fill of ripe persimmons.
Another day, my brother took his hatchet
to the two dark-wooded trees
and felled them both.
I watched as he dismembered them,
stripped the trunks and limbs of bark.
When Dad appeared,
my brother fled into the woods.
Dad swore. He stood silent
by the fallen trees, head down,
mouth moving as in prayer.
Side by side, we rolled the last persimmons
into piles then crouched beside them,
squeezed each tiny fruit—
some green and dry, some ripe,
some far too soft to save.

# DEACONS MEETING

Five men smoke outside the convenience store
that doesn't exactly have a name. Over the door
hangs a sign: COLD BEER CHEAP GAS.
The men smell of hay and cow and hot skin.
Two perch on a tailgate, their boots
barely scraping the gravel.
One wears a damp red hat and he lifts it
to wipe sweat from his balding skull with a rag.
The one in the white t-shirt swears
and says, *hell hath no fury like a woman's scorn,
that's what the Bible says*, and the one
beside him disagrees, reckons it's not even in the Bible.
*The hell it ain't*, the other says, because he knows
it's a good one and all the good ones
come from the Bible. The sun pours out wet heat
like a steam engine and the ground
radiates and the hood of the truck shines dully,
reflecting in the eyes of a hound
whose tongue lolls and who hogs
the only bit of shadow cast by an old turnkey
Coke machine. The older one gets to explaining
how that ain't necessarily so when high above
in the hot sky a jet breaks the sound barrier
with a jarring crack and the five men and the dog
crane their necks upward to figure out
where exactly it's flying to. *I bet that sumbitch
is headed to Warner Robins*, one of them says.
*Naw that's north it's headed*, says another,
*I betcha it's headed to Chattanooga*,
and the shirtless one with the stubbled jowl
who has until now been silent
figures it's about damn time they talked about
something else besides women.

# TAKE, EAT

*...this is my body.* —Matthew 26:26

We skimmed the bottom of Duck Creek for crawdads,
sifted through the silt with our fingers,
felt the cool rush of fright as the tiny claws curled around us.

We held them up to the low light,
saw the glinting points of reflection,
shell the color of Georgia mud.

My brother grasped the heads between his fingers,
pinched them off with a wet pop, strung them as bait on his line.
We carried the bodies home with the few small fish we'd caught.

I had never eaten crawdad before.
Our neighbor fished them from a boiling pot with tongs,
husked them of their shells, soft as infant fingernails.

The tail meat floated in a pool of butter,
the white muscle curling in on itself.

I ran from the house into the pine thicket,
kicked pine needles into muddy heaps.

I leaned hard on a tree as thin as a cow tail,
stepped on the trunk, waited for the damp snap,
the acid gasp of its breaking.

## II.

# JAROSLAV SEIFERT PRAYING

*Prague, August 21, 1968*

O Lord,
I left you in my boyhood.
But this morning
the horizon cracked open
and tanks poured
into my city.

Russians filled
the streets below my window
and I drank
belts of slivovice
straight from the bottle.
The telephone rang.
On the other end I heard
my friend laughing.
They'd smashed his Leica
with their rifle butts.

I have worshipped
poetry and my homeland
and I am not ashamed.
Czechoslovakia is lost.
If they kill me
I will wear my blue suit
with buttons bright
as Mother Slava's eyes.

But I am a little drunk.
Lord, though you can't hear,
deliver us from our enemies.
Let us open like the sea
and swallow them up.

# MARTIN, SLOVAKIA

As the elevator door ticked shut, my neighbor
Villam lurched in and, red-faced, gripped my arm
and chortled, "Pivko, pivko," taking pulls
from a mimed bottle—*beer, a little beer.*

My Slovak too rough for a polite decline,
I let him drag me down the ice-slicked block.
Inside the corner potraviny, Villam dropped
two euros on the counter, shoved a lukewarm

bottle in my hands—"Pi, pi." (*Drink, drink.*)
Villam was old. His face was old. He stank
of sweat, and bacon grease, and borovička.
I think he lived alone (I lived alone),

and I couldn't understand a thing he slurred
except, "môj syn, môj syn"—*My son, my son.*

# MORAVIA

*for my father*

In this city whose name you can't pronounce—
where women pace barefoot in dry grass and rusting
bottle caps, sandals in hands, skirts trailing for days;
where old men pack grocery aisles, tens of them, alone,
palming blocks of Edam; where flower-sellers, mustached,
slick-haired, silk ties cinched tightly, flit restaurant to restaurant
like rumors, roses spilling from their arms, pockets full of coins,
while outside, street kids release firecrackers from paper shrouds;
where paraders roam squares, scarves waving,
whose chants rise even as the bottles fall to stone;
where girls in wooden fair-booths, eyes study-weary
beneath the ridiculous haberdashery of corporate America,
slice salami for bankers and tourists and the hungry poor
with soiled bills outstretched—I think of you.
You told me once you'd rather do without all that,
that you'd only ever have one home and that wasn't it,
that you'd never call this home, said you'd never
lost anything here. Home is the place we lose things:
daylight hunched over engines and their elegies
to oil, the decades of dust; money year after year
bailing your boys out of jail in towns with names
familiar as worn flannel; sleep, teeth (one to an apple,
one to a walnut you find nestled in black leaves
behind a church); your fear of losing me every time
I return to feel your stubble against my cheek.
Here, thousands of birds on spires and antennae
raise their terrible throats to the morning
as though they'd never met. Right now
I am alone in a train car with a girl you'll never know,
and as we idle at a border crossing, eyeing each other's passports
for the first time, she gives me handfuls of radishes,
and I know I will lose her, lose whole days pacing alleys
in the cobbled pastels of this city I will also lose,
which will become, as I speed away from it, my home.

# PRAYER

Forget the factory town's sooty snow
on your tongue in an open square
at night, and us in it.
Forget the vagrants with their fake folk ballads
and the coins we threw to them.
Forget the long trains
and the deep red apples you pulled from your bag,
placing them into my cupped hands.
Forget the smell of sour cream and dumpling flour,
of boots and damp grass
in your house behind the station
where you knelt by your bed
scrubbing wine from threadbare carpet.
Forget the cut of my coat.
Forget the books I brought you.
If you have to, please, forget the drizzly night in Prague
we saw a man swing a bottle
like a ballplayer, split it into shards
on another man's cheekbone,
his body pitching back into the arms of smoking strangers.
Forget that he didn't yelp, that he didn't even cry out,
though it's true the music held us in its pulse
and I couldn't hear myself hum,
couldn't hear you speak,
couldn't have told, no matter how hard I strained,
that the band was playing a sad song,
that the singer wasn't laughing into the microphone,
wasn't promising us, as you gripped my arm,
that we would be alright.
Forget my name if you have to.
Forget the spired churches like bus terminals,
and how our bodies pressed against each other,
against those gathered for mass, for vespers.

# FOREIGNERS

I.

The Bible tells us
something like: *Do not
awaken love
until it so desires.*

As though we ever have a choice in it.

But Solomon was king
and wiser than I'll ever be.
He had hundreds of wives
and concubines

yet no one ever held him
fully captive.

Maybe he was lucky—

never once
to see a woman drenched

in neon light
at a Czech train station bar

as thin smoke curls up
from her mouth,

or walk with her,
close but never touching,
through empty cities

tasting all her different names:
*Karol, Karolina, Karolinka,*

*moja.*

II.

*Brno, Czech Republic*

We met beneath the clock
on Česká Street as bodies poured
from trams.

Karolina—till then only a name
and mobile number—held out
her hand for mine.

Her English, frail
as glass and thick with Czech
and Irish tones,

rang inside me like a distant bell.

She wanted me

to take the words she'd learned
in Ireland—her year as an *au pair*—

and make them new,
and more,
and bigger than they'd been.

I couldn't. Now I think
we both knew that.

Just what we taught
each other is still
hard to discern.

III.

Karolina's name among her friends
was *krtek*, the mole.

Gender: masculine. I could almost see it.

Like the animal, she was small,
her hair a short, black tuft of spikes
that gleamed
and blued in softer light,

but that was all,
the whole of the resemblance.

Her deep-set eyes could look
through walls and men
and tear down both.
And though her hands

were broad with nails
trimmed short,

they held a glass or cigarette
with tenderness,
a surgeon's curiosity.

I envied everything she touched with them.

Were I the earth, I'd wish
she were the mole.

*Burrow deep*, I'd say. *Be happy.*

*Stay.*

IV.

I slipped in late and took a seat
beside Karolina
in the flickering dark.

The cinema was cold
and almost empty,

though Karol's arm
pressed hotly into mine.

The dialog was Shakespeare's original
with the Czech subtitles I knew
she would need.

I struggled to make sense of either one.

*The Merchant of Venice.*
I'd never read the play

but knew it was a tragic comedy.

And that was us—
two people in the dark
together,
acting out two different scripts.

Mine, in English, barely overlapped
with hers. We'd gasp

or sigh at different times,
touch skin to skin, lock eyes
then look away.

V.

The man she'd loved,
she said, was from Brazil—

a handyman turned
Irish butcher's aide with skin
as smooth as černé pivo.

She spoke no Portuguese.
He spoke no Czech.

They patched their love together
out of scraps of English, out of sweat

commingled
in his flat above the meat shop.

She said only a foreigner
can make a girl
as crazy as she felt back then.

I knew exactly what she meant.

My hands shook
as I rolled a skinny cigarette.

Karolina plucked it
from my fingers,

lit it with a match,
and smirked at me.

*You're bad for me,* she said,

lips barely parting.

VI.

*When you speak a language,
dream in it,*

*from birth, I mean, your heart
can speak it, too.*

*Brazilian guy, I loved him,
but his heart
spoke different language.*

*That is how world works.*

*Only Czech guy understands
Czech woman.*

*This is true. I learned it more than once.*

*Maybe you don't believe,
but you will see,
and I don't want it for you.
Stay away.*

*From love, I mean.*

*You should save the love
for someone else—American girl.*

*My heart, foreign guy
can never understand.
Man who tries to translate will get hurt.*

*For example, you.*

*You must dream in your language,
I must dream in mine.*

VII.

*Albertina Museum, Vienna*

I lost her
on the second floor,

just past the stairs
she'd mounted hurriedly
to find the Edvard Munch.

I saw her disappear into the crowd.

She always was too quick
for me, and that day,

Karolina
energized by art
and Turkish coffee,

I didn't stand a chance.

Perhaps I never really did.
Her mind
was always elsewhere—

another crowded hall,
another room I didn't quite belong in.

I found her peering
deep into a painting,

her body

framed in gold, enraptured, alone.

VIII.

Karolina rummaged
through her bag and brought out
sacks of apples,
radishes, sweet corn and pears.

I never felt less Czech
or less alone
than when she fed me there—

the train compartment
empty but for us—
idling at Vienna Südbahnhof.

Soon the train would speed us
toward Moravia, her home

and not quite mine.

She slouched across from me
and chewed a radish,

her bare feet
crossed and balanced on my knee.

Outside, a whistle trilled.
I knew she'd never love a foreigner again.

But there, we both were

still *Ausländeren,*

the border looming
somewhere far ahead.

# INTRODUCTION TO CZECH STUDIES

*Brno, Czech Republic*

In a pub off Veveři street, the linguistics professor,
sweating, neckerchiefed, rails that Kundera
still comes to visit the city, though in disguise.
We know this to be false. At least that's what we hope.
We don't want to imagine him in a fake mustache,
wide-brimmed hat pulled low, refusing to speak.

We have all been drinking. The professor peeks
at us through his fingers, the sobering process
beginning already. He says it was a sad mistake,
Kundera's exile. Inside the man had lived a chimera—
part socialism, part artist's temper, part dope.
It had been the seventies after all. We discuss

his plight, wondering how one might disguise
oneself to return home in secret. One's speech
must surely modulate—a new accent, the loping
intonation of a foreigner. He grew progressively
more French with each year away, and so Kundera,
by now, would not need the thin mustache

we pray he never penciled on. The man must act
lost and foreign with ease, flawlessly disgusted
by the locals. The professor mimes a camera
with his fingers. He tells us that Kundera speaks
English in the shops like a tourist, and might profess
his love for France in Freedom Square. We hope

he is mistaken. The professor does not cope
well with slivovice. He admits drinking is a mistake
for a man like him—a sad, washed-up protestor.
All those years damning the Marxists he despised
wore him down. Now only two things make him speak
his true mind: hard plum liquor, and Kundera.

The Czechoslovakia of his mind is its own chimera—
part mother's milk, part hopelessness, part hope.
He's never seen Silesia or the Tatras' peaks,
but he's climbed library stacks, knows the musty, ashen
corners of every church beneath gray Moravian skies,
knows Kundera—his fallen star—and us, his confessors.

# NOT RECOGNIZING THE STONE IS A LION

The people of the village
mill past it every morning
and they carry on their backs
bundles of kindling and pig
fat and sometimes their babies.
Old men perch on the stone
to rest and they lay their canes
across their laps like rifles.
Winter, the stone slicked
by snow. Boys reckon
the tactics of a snowball fight.
Spring, and girls tug
their sweethearts by the wrists
to kiss them under cherry blossoms.
They do this every year.
The girls do this so they will remain
tender and their wombs will open
like a cannon's mouth.
They do not recognize the stone is a lion.
They do not know that by summer
they will hang limp from its jaws,
the dust still settling on the road to Warsaw.

# BENEDICTION FOR SLOVAKIA

*Numbers 6:24–26*

Bless Jozef Ruman and the house his sons
moved home to build with him, the mother dead
ten years, and bless the sweating cups of ice
and young white wine the three men palm together,
silent, the floorboards settling beneath them.

Bless Villam Ondrla who, half-drunk, shovels
snow and watches families traipse sure-footed
down the lanes he cleared. Lord, bless the sons
he never had, the wife he'll never lose,
his bare apartment. Bless them, Father, keep them.

Bless the Roma children dotting sidewalks
everywhere, all coatless, laughing, flinging
rocks at gutted, crumbling tenements
circling the train yard. Bless their idle hands.
Father, turn your face to shine upon them.

Bless all the men who've seen more flags than most
men ever see unfurled above their streets—
and bless the fading Hapsburg-era glamour
of flaking gold foil, plaster cracked and soot stained,
the spired cathedrals empty, wreathed in lichen.

Lord, Bless the towering blocks of pre-fab flats—
their fuchsias, ochres, pastel blues, and yellows
where the Communist grays and whites had been—
and bless the singer on the street proclaiming
"Slováci ožijú"—*the Slovaks will revive.*

III.

# ISAIAH

With blistered lips and tongue I prophesied
the coming fire, the blight, the trampled vineyard,
the kingdom overrun.
                        Looking inward,
I'd seen the nightmares of my heart collide—
seen famine, my people in captivity
while I, my condemnation wrought in verse,
was too unclean to speak. And even worse,
I'd seen my name fall to obscurity.

I placed the coal upon my lips—I'd say
an angel did—to cleanse me of the wrongs
for which my unwashed people burned.
                                      With songs
of grape and ash, I gathered scribes and preached—
through bandages—the price they'd have to pay.
They trembled. That's how deep in them I reached.

# FORGIVENESS

When I say that I hate you, I say it
like Beethoven hunched over crisp staff paper,
the clean lines accusing him
and the pitiful vibration of the floorboards,
the piano flat upon them as he hammered out
odes to the things he lost.
Like a fisherman breathing cool sea air,
his nets empty another season.
Like a sexton in an empty church, pushing his broom
over spotless floors for the third time this morning.
Like a mother to the bottle as her child
first lifts it to his own clumsy lips.
Like Napoleon to the delicate scent
of soap on his wife's neck before sex.
Yes, I hate you like a hunter hates the deer
that finally didn't get away, like a vintner hates
the grapes too dark and sweet to crush,
how he places them one by one on his own tongue,
eyes shut tight against the morning.
First the musk of the peel and then the flesh—
the tingle of it rising in his cheeks.

# PESSIMIST'S GUIDE TO MIRACLES

A donkey in Siena brays the name
of Catherine, his saint, but no one hears—
no Balaam to be spared the angel's flame.

How many miracles pass by this same
irreverent way? We're sleeping off our beers
some Sunday while a donkey prays the name

of some Italian saint. We watch the game,
the infomercials' half-time racketeers,
flipping past the preachers' sulfur, wrath, and flame,

all while the donkey's keeper, in bed with shame—
with someone else's wife—gondoliers
his way to hell, moaning the vessel's name.

The donkey's voice is sweet as aspartame
and Catherine leans down to rub his ears.
We're blind to her, we Balaams, blind to flame,

but hey: we die. We all do. Life is lame.
Miracles can't save us from our fears—
a whirlwind singing its next victim's name,
a storm-split oak, a farmhouse wreathed in flame.

# ST. NICHOLAS OF LYCIA, DEFENDER OF ORTHODOXY, WONDERWORKER

In Turkey they scarcely knew my name—
*Father*, they called me. *Bishop*. And every day
they came to me one by one and spilled
their sins in the dark, spat their own damnation
through the slot, my dim face on the other side.
The other priests were the worst.
*Forgive me, Father, I dream of her on my mouth*
*like grapes, wake to the taste of wine.*
They never asked me if I wanted their sins,
never asked my name, but I took them all
nonetheless, baked loaves for the poor
from the heat of them, scattered them
like rye seed over the rectory's sandy garden.
When the famine came, they slowly forsook me,
their stomachs too empty to sin. Only the butcher
still came to confess. Every day he entered my booth
to offload himself, the load a little bigger each time.
*Forgive me, Father, I have doubted.*
*Forgive me, I have fornicated in my heart,*
*with my hands. Father, I am hungry.*
When he told me of the three little boys,
how he split their flesh from bone with his cleaver,
laid them in salt to cure like swine, I knew
there could be no forgiveness for me, for him,
for any of us. I tore my vestment from my body,
ran bare-chested into the streets purpled by dusk.
Inside the butcher's shop I laid hands on the barrel
of boy meat and brine, plunged them into
its cooling depths, felt their names on my skin,
I swear I did. People like to say I prayed for the boys,
that I cinched my sainthood in a matter of seconds,
three miracles in one as the boys sprang from the barrel
clean and whole and blinking like new foals.

# CZAR NICHOLAS THE BLOODY

Round and round on the floor we would go,
my father and I, roughhousing like peasants
as my mother watched and clicked her tongue
in her soft Danish way, shaking her head
as we swore and scuffled and laughed
through the happy pain of it all.
When he pinned me, finally, and he always did,
I would bury my face in the damp linen
of his chest, breathing in his cologne
that stank of cedar and crushed cherry blossoms.
I always envied his strength as he tore
an orange from its rind, or drew his bow
across the violin his hands swallowed,
or looked straight in the eyes of foreign men
in long black coats and told them *No*.
Summers, we would trade Petrograd
for Finland's forest manors, and some mornings
my father would take the axe from our servant,
laying his own weight into the firewood
as I watched from the salon window.
When they made me Czar, I draped
my daughters in diamonds no assassin's bullet
could break, ran my hands hard down
the banisters of our Winter Palace until they blistered.

# NICOLAS OF ANTIOCH, THE PROSELYTE

*Acts 6–7*

We were waiters, the seven of us,
anointed by Peter and the others

to feed the wives of martyred Greeks.
Stephen was our leader, and how beautiful

he was. His beard gleamed like smelted copper
in the sun as we gathered wheat.

His shoulders moved like a weaver's
hands beneath his thin white robe.

I thought of the old stories, of Leda
taking the swan's warm, firm neck

in her hands and laying it across her lap.
I thought of feathers on damp skin,

the honk and flap of urgent love,
her tongue trailing the curve of his beak.

Mornings I watched as Stephen stirred
heaps of ash and coal to wake the fires

within the hearths we'd built together
from mud and clay and days of sweat.

When they killed him, I crouched among the stones
to hold him, kissed the place his face had been.

# NICHOLAS COPERNICUS

I wanted to wrap myself in the crisp green
of the priesthood, feel the gentle bend of the host

before its breaking. I wanted to open myself
like a scroll and cant the ancient algorithms

of salt and oil, of vinegar and blood and forgiveness.
I wanted to fill gilded halls with homiletics

and whisper absolution in the dark.
But the tilt of the sky turning above me

seemed too imperfect, the slope of the stars
along the horizon bent too sharply toward the earth.

How my hands shook as I raised the astrolabe
and spun its dial—how damp with sweat

the parchment I scribbled equations onto.
Nights, in fields like open doors, I turned my ear upward

to hear the stars' confessions: *We are distant, we are vast.*
*Forgive us, Father, though we burn already.*

# THE LAST SHEEP IN UZ

*Job 1:13–22*

While clouds of roiling fire rolled in and fell
to earth, disintegrating all my kin,
I was already lonesome, growing thin
and sick at heart. It should have hurt like hell

to watch them burn—the stench of melted wool
hanging in the air—or made me trot
with joy at my escape, but it did not.
Life, at last, spares no one. I'm no fool.

Since I was just a lamb I've seen men slit
our throats and throw us wholly on the fire
in penitence, and a week ago yesterday

I watched them place my mother bit by bit
into their savage maws and smile. I tire
of waiting. Oh, that they'd come for me today.

# SOMETHING ELSE

*Something else*, my grandmother said,
as in, *those boys down by the creek are*

*something else* or *Reverend, that sermon
was something else*, and I couldn't stop

thinking that it was our fault: the bees
now distant, as though they had lumbered

across the cold shallows of Styx, shaking
their fur for the boatman dozing at the rudder.

Later, when scientists offered an explanation,
disease of bees on a biblical scale, the Reverend

offered his prayer to the black flecks of a failing
sky, pollen sacs laden and glistening. Somehow

we knew it was something else entirely,
warm, measurable as honey—the flowers

by the walkway straining toward each other
though they just couldn't reach.

# OF SOLOMON

Beloved:
    *Lover, dark as I may be*
*from picking sun-sweet, nectar-heavy fruit*
*in other vineyards, give yourself to me.*
*My bed is fertile. Tend my withered root.*

Lover:
    *Mind your fruit, your drooping vines.*
*I've seen whole packs of foxes stalking through*
*your open gates. Catch them. Crush their spines.*
*Forget them. Then I'll give myself to you.*

Beloved:
    *I was in the streets all night,*
*helpless to my body's single need.*

Lover:
    *I was busy drinking starlight*
*through my skin—the wheat fields thick with seed.*

Friends:
    *If love's a cellar, bolt the door.*
*If love's an apple, bite it to the core.*

# SAMSON IN LOVE

*...out of the strong came forth sweetness.* —Judges 14:14

He always imagined grasping
his father's blade, running it hard

down his own scalp and jaw as his hair fell
about his feet in messy piles.

He thought of plunging his arms
elbow-deep in the wine jars,

rubbing the bitterness into his skin
until his hands were pruned with violet.

When he saw the Philistine girl,
he swore he knew how he would end,

swore there would be whole days
dozing naked in empty fields,

his head resting in the small of her back,
her shoulder blades looming in his eyes

like Zion and Arafat, and as he climbed them
with his fingertips he'd dream

of God transfigured and wake to it.

# AN EMAIL FROM GOD CONCERNING THE RECENT PLAGUE OF LOCUSTS

*And there came out of the smoke locusts upon the earth:
and unto them was given power.* —Revelation 9:3

Yesterday I twisted open the cap of the world
and in flowed locusts—tiny centurions,
breasts bronzed with armor, their forelegs clanging
together like swords upon shields.
They twisted through the clouds like lightning.
You saw them crashing toward you
and I noticed you clenched your laptop

to your chest as if you thought they were rain.
You reminded me of Pharaoh cradling his son's limp body
in his arms, cursing me as though I were a motorist
who had run the boy over and driven away.
But you ducked into a Starbucks before the locusts hit
and all hell quite literally broke loose. As you sat
sipping your latte and typing on your screenplay,

I watched the locusts strip bark from trees,
paint from houses, stacks of letters from the hands
of postmen, and then the postmen themselves,
their uniforms collapsing into small blue heaps,
which the locusts then devoured. You may not have seen
the swarm invade the pet shop. They swirled
like the great clouds of a tornado and ate and ate

until the animals were merely white cages
locked in larger cages, the shopkeeper's bones
slumped over the counter. You seemed not to appreciate
their sweep through the bus station, leaving in their wake
only watches, wallets, and here and there
a prosthetic limb, the buses idling emptily in their lanes.
Once they had eaten their fill, I watched as they spiraled

back up into the atmosphere, the black mass of them
blotting out the sun so that you thought it was night
already and decided to head home for a bite.
I know you were pissed that you had to walk
all that way in the dark, but I did notice that locusts
figure prominently into the end of Act II Scene VII
and I wanted to say, *you're welcome.*

# THE APOCALYPSE BLAHS

*And the third angel sounded, and there fell a great star from heaven, burning as it were a lamp, and it fell upon the third part of the rivers, and upon the fountains of waters.* —Revelation 8:10

Today we are less than industrious.
Stars fall around us and we read the morning
paper by their flaming out. STARS FALL.

PRESIDENT TOO BORED TO COMMENT.
How banal, we think, this anemic rain of fire.
Thousands of years ago, we spotted stars going

nova despite our small means to cope. We were
scientists then, squatting in piles of bones
to record the skies on cave rock. We sang

to their dying—threw our bodies into one
another, tore our hair, held up offerings
of meat and hide. With pigments from soil,

we painted ourselves with starbursts,
built monuments that stretched toward heaven
like midday flowers. Today, with less conviction

than on most days, daytime TV actors
cough their lines, gazing past the camera
to the coffee machine. In front of our TVs,

we are all layered in fine dust.
We have forgotten to pick our children
up from preschool. We have forgotten leaves

under our feet that will melt into the soil
like a lover. In the swell of the land's darkness,
we have forgotten the light in heaven's

windows, how when it falls, it burns up
the land and how, even in their burning,
trees cling wildly to the earth.

# ORPHEUS IN HUNTSVILLE, ALABAMA

My mama, godly as she was,
never forgave my daddy for quitting
the church. For politics. She couldn't.
She'd always wanted to marry a preacher,
and married one, but then he ran
for mayor and won. The king of Huntsville.

Years later, when her mind was gone,
she told me how he'd lay her down,
his fingers circling her bellybutton,
breathe the scripture into her neck—
*Thy navel is like a round goblet
which wanteth not liquor*—and take her
with biblical authority.
She said that, once he'd shed the cloth,
his touch no longer felt the same.
How could it? He forsook the Spirit.

Now both of them are long buried.
But daddy taught me the fiddle, and mama
sang her hymns so sweet they shimmied
out her throat and into mine.

# SEMINARIAN AT THE PREACHERS' CONVENTION

Will no one listen to my little song?
We chat, we nod—but nothing's ever heard.
Perhaps I won't be with you very long.

I know all Jesus preached on right and wrong—
I croon the Psalms and Proverbs like a bird,
though you've already heard this ancient song.

Through conference rooms, I pull myself along
and sip a lonely ginger ale—my third.
I may well not be with you very long.

My voice and solemn handshake: both are strong
from practice tending someone else's herd,
but no one listens to my little song.

I've shown up late—I'll have to fight a throng
to hear the keynote speaker teach the Word.
I don't think I'll be with you very long.

I want someone to tell me, *you belong,
son—rave on like the Prophets, undeterred,*
but no one seems to hear my desperate song.
I think that I'll move on before too long.

# NOTES

"The Name Museum": I am indebted to my friend Joshua Gottlieb-Miller for the title of this poem and, as such, the title of this collection.

"Psalm 137": The italicized portions of lines 5–6 are from "The Old Rugged Cross," a Methodist hymn written by George Bennard in 1912.

"Beheaded Carcass of a Deer": This poem borrows much of its structure from Stephen Mitchell's translation of "Archaic Torso of Apollo" by Rainer Maria Rilke.

"Foreigners": The italicized portions of lines 2–4 are from Song of Solomon 2:7. All biblical quotations in this collection are taken from the King James Version.

"Benediction for Slovakia": The phrase "Slováci ožijú" is a refrain from "Nad Tatrou sa blýska," the Slovak national anthem.

"Orpheus in Huntsville, Alabama": The italicized portions of lines 11–12 are from Song of Solomon 7:2.

"Seminarian at the Preachers' Convention": The refrains here began as lines from "At the Party" by W.H. Auden.

# ACKNOWLEDGMENTS

Grateful acknowledgment is made to the editors of the publications in which many of these poems first appeared:

*American Literary Review*: "Apple," "Forgiveness," "Czar Nicholas the Bloody"
*Birmingham Poetry Review*: "For the Robinson Brothers of Chattooga County, Georgia, Now Deceased," "Mountain Redemption," "Joseph Van Gilreath (1924–1991)," "Genesis," "The Last Sheep in Uz"
*Copper Nickel*: "The Name Museum," "St. Nicholas of Lycia, Defender of Orthodoxy, Wonderworker"
*Country Dog Review*: "Gutting the Farmhouse Upon Grandfather's Death from Alzheimer's"
*Hayden's Ferry Review*: "Psalm 137"
*iO*: "Beheaded Carcass of a Deer"
*Iron Horse Literary Review*: "Drawl"
*Linebreak*: "Moravia"
*Mead*: "Killing a Rattler"
*Old Red Kimono*: "Seminarian at the Preachers' Convention"
*Passages North*: "Prayer"
*Poet Lore*: "Take, Eat" (as "Initiation")
*Relief*: "Pessimist's Guide to Miracles," "Nicholas Copernicus"
*Revolution House*: "Introduction to Czech Studies," "Benediction for Slovakia," "Martin, Slovakia"
*Scythe*: "Samson in Love," "Deacons Meeting"
*Southern Review*: "Thanatophobia on Shinbone Valley Road"
*Stirring*: "Cozy Manor Personal Care Home, LaFayette, Georgia," "Nicolas of Antioch, the Proselyte," "Something Else," "The Apocalypse Blahs"
*storySouth*: "Persimmon"
*Sweet*: "An Email from God Concerning the Recent Plague of Locusts"
*Third Coast*: "Isaiah"
*Unsplendid*: "Orpheus in Huntsville, Alabama," "Of Solomon"
*Vinyl Poetry*: "The Emigrant's Son"
*Willows Wept Review*: "Not Recognizing the Stone Is a Lion"

"Jaroslav Seifert Praying" first appeared in *Two Weeks: A Digital Anthology of Contemporary Poetry* (Linebreak, 2011). Several of these poems appear in the chapbook *Mountain Redemption* (Black Lawrence Press, 2014).

Heartfelt gratitude to Chad Davidson, Andrew Hudgins, and Eric Smith, who made this book what it is, and to Daniel Anderson, Henri Cole, Caitlin Doyle, Claudia Emerson, Alex Fabrizio, Kathy Fagan, Greg Fraser, Joshua Gottlieb-Miller, Mark Jarman, Thomas Lux, Emilia Phillips, Wyatt Prunty, Dave Smith, Analicia Sotelo, Matt Sumpter, Sidney Wade, G.C. Waldrep, and the many others without whose friendship, patience, generosity, and keen eyes and ears these poems would not have been possible.

Special thanks to Vivian Shipley for selecting this book for the De Novo Poetry Prize, and to Chad Prevost, Ryan G. Van Cleave, John Estes, and the rest of C&R Press for their confidence in my work.

I am grateful to the U.S. Department of State and the J. William Fulbright Program, the Bucknell Seminar for Younger Poets, Sewanee Writers' Conference, the University of West Georgia, and The Ohio State University for the generous grants and fellowships that blessed me with the time and resources to bring these poems into being.

My undying love to my family.

www.ingramcontent.com/pod-product-compliance
Lightning Source LLC
Chambersburg PA
CBHW021025090426
**42738CB00007B/903**